In the Enemy Camp

William Wantling

In the Enemy Camp

Selected poems 1964-74

with an introduction by **John Osborne**
& foreword by **Thurston Moore**

Tangerine Press

• 2015 •

ISBN 978-0-9573385-7-9 (paperback)
   978-0-9573385-8-6 (hardback)

IN THE ENEMY CAMP. © 2015 RUTHIE WANTLING
INTRODUCTION. © 2015 JOHN OSBORNE
FOREWORD. © 2015 THURSTON MOORE
FIRST PUBLISHED 2015 BY TANGERINE PRESS
18 RIVERSIDE ROAD
GARRATT BUSINESS PARK
LONDON
SW17 0BA
ENGLAND
eatmytangerine.com
PRINTED & BOUND IN ENGLAND
ALL RIGHTS RESERVED

Printed on 100% recycled, acid-free paper.

Publisher's Note
& Acknowledgements

THIS BOOK is intended to be a definitive selection of Wantling's poetic output from when he begun publishing work in 1964 – a year after his release from prison – up to his untimely death in May 1974. All previous collections, magazine and anthology contributions have been consulted, including a manuscript of *From the Jungle's Edge*, which the publisher came across by chance in Wantling's archive. This collection was scheduled for publication by Swallow Press, but was shelved indefinitely following the death of Alan Swallow in 1966. Many of those poems are included herein. Tangerine Press has published Wantling's work in a variety of limited editions, including *Only in the Sun* and *The Fix*, a two volume celebration from 2008. Both of those books are long out of print, making the poems in the present volume readily available for the first time to a wider audience.

There are many people to thank for making this book possible: John Osborne; Thurston Moore; Alan Dent; Ian Seed; Trevor Reeves, for allowing me to see his extensive archive on that memorable visit to Dunedin, New Zealand in 2007; Peter Olds; Adrian Manning; Jim Burns; Kevin Jones; Kevin Ring; Carol Peluso; Jeffrey Weinberg; Bill McLean and Greg Koos of McLean County Museum of History, Bloomington, Illinois for archive access and assistance; Chris Harter, for the extensive list of Wantling's contributions to various obscure magazines. Specific acknowledgement must go to all the editors of the original books, pamphlets, literary magazines and anthologies, from which this selection has been made, especially: Kirby Congdon, Marvin Malone, Erik Kiviat, Douglas Blazek, Walter Lowenfels, Alan Swallow, Len Fulton, Bernard Stone, Edward Lucie-Smith, Peter Finch, Trevor Reeves, A.D. Winans, James Callahan. Finally, an extra special thank you goes to Ruthie Wantling, for her unwavering support, encouragement and generosity of spirit from day one.

MICHAEL CURRAN
LONDON, ENGLAND

Table of Contents

Foreword

THE ASPECT OF POETRY IN ROCK N' ROLL entered a remarkable phase in the mid to late 1970s. Post-Dylan, Lou Reed, Neil Young et al, there arose a new nihilist activist voice of punk rock with writers, both in song and in poetry. People of dark mystery and wan visage, wearing black and drifting through city streets, making a racket to confound and chase away any overstayed hippie idealism, be it burnt out or just lost in dope nod. Poets like Patti Smith, certainly, espousing beat bards Allen Ginsberg, William Burroughs, Gregory Corso as well as expressing a heart fluttering fascination with Arthur Rimbaud and his French Symbolist outliers. And Jim Carroll, young and pretty and pacing his fast words on the page with considered regard to the previous New York Schools of Ted Berrigan and Frank O'Hara and still finding some glorious moments to get high and do nothing. Both Richard Hell and Tom Verlaine, founders of poet rock band Television (nee The Neon Boys), whose surnames referenced the same romance Patti had with Rimbaud and the gang, had published minimalist poems of off-wit and desire, with connective thought to poets recently lost in the culture of consumer America, from Bill Knott to Ron Padgett to d.a. levy to Richard Krech to Bill Bissett.

Women poets were not silent but it was these male voices, sometimes tough and ugly and lit-genreized as Meat Poets, yet hardly afraid of exhibiting emotion historically applied to femininity, that spoke of a post WWII consciousness. One where, by the advent of punk rock fuse-lighting, the 1950s/60s counter culture heraldry could be infernoed then swept into the bin so the contempo-punk youth could pogo to an all-new everything-is-permitted future. Through the lens of these punk poets we could trace some strange lineage of underground action, mostly existing in ephemeral states of small press, mimeographed, region specific and with no realistic ambition but to communicate with like minded purveyors of dream desire, domestic anxiety, sensual melancholia and a shared genius of the artists life and its glory of romance and poverty.

Discovering the writing of William Wantling amidst the environment of American underground poetry of the 1960s was like discovering a lost fuzz rock psychedelic stoner loner LP by a band from Peoria, Illinois (where Wantling resided most of his life) released in a very limited pressing and completely overshadowed by the commercial bunk of the time. Archiving poetry books by wild hair head poets like d.a. levy from Cleveland, Ohio or *The Willie* from parts unknown, and gleaning the mindset of truly anti-authoritarian Vietnam era free-thinkers, it was entirely thrilling to catch wind of William Wantling and to locate his chapbooks *Down, Off & Out* (Mimeo Press, USA 1965), *Obscene & Other Poems* (Caveman Press, New Zealand 1972), *Sick Fly* and *10,000 r.p.m. & Digging It, Yeah!* (Second Aeon, UK 1970, 1973 respectively) to name a few. His pages exhibited an energy and concision that spoke of dark 4ams in junk stasis and errant emotion, and of a youth spent in combat, which would always define a hard specificity in his brain and heart. But, like the beauty and grace of the community of Beat, post-Beat, Bardo, Meat etc poets of his age, there is a belief in art reflecting beauty and the enchantment of nature and cosmology.

The man passed away in 1974 probably without a thought to his value as a poet, a great poet, in any critical regard. But as we share these pages, pamphlets, books, this particular anthology, his work continues to have a sentient effect for the very real reason of how great it was.

THURSTON MOORE
LONDON, ENGLAND

William Wantling, Neglected Master

LIKE MANY ANOTHER WAR VET, convict and heroin addict, William Wantling (1933-74) was possessed by demons; his greatness is to have wrestled those demons until they sang. Born in Peoria, Illinois, shortly before the comedian Richard Pryor (their careers share affinities), Wantling's formative experiences of the Great Depression, the Second World War, the Cold War, the conflicts in Korea and Vietnam, the Civil Rights movement and the omnipresent threat of nuclear armageddon put him thoroughly at odds with everything the town epitomized. 'Will it play in Peoria?', meaning 'how will it go down on Main Street?', is a catch-phrase associated with conservative politicians such as John D. Ehrlichman, Richard Nixon, Ronald Reagan and George W. Bush. Our title poem, 'In the Enemy Camp', hilariously critiques Silent Majority conformism by listing its repressions: no Jazz, no casual clothes, no casual sex, no drugs, a population so docile that the police can afford to be polite, and a black community that 'knows its place'. The poem is set in Peoria: the Enemy Camp is home town. The use of humour in this and other satirical poems like 'it was 5 am' and '*Who's* Bitter?' demonstrates Wantling's poetic tact: knowing that nothing is more anti-authoritarian than laughter, he deploys it to obviate preachiness, laughing down the walls of Jericho. As we shall see, comedy is only one colour in his palette.

Wantling's elegies for the likes of Caryl Chessman, Billie Holiday, Lenny Bruce, Lester Young and James Dean identify him as existential outsider, Norman Mailer's 'white negro', a rebel *with* a cause. His life can be read as an oedipally driven flight from all forms of patriarchal power, though one that led him to embrace things – military conflict, hard drugs, crime, marital failure, absentee fatherhood, prostitution – that inevitably made him complicitous with what he condemned. His poetry acknowledges the guilt. Those moments in which his narrators confess to murder, theft or heroin-user's loss of libido –

> I taught my wife to masturbate
> so I could sleep more
> or at least lay there
> & stare at the wall

> She cries while she does it

are profoundly affecting, gravid with contrition:

> what I wouldn't
> give to go back, to
> start all over

They also carry a political charge, the acknowledgement of personal culpability deepening the condemnation of the dominant society for refusing to do the same. As Wantling's favourite novelist Albert Camus puts it in *La Chute* (*The Fall*), 'we cannot assert the innocence of anyone, whereas we can state with certainty the guilt of all'.

True to form, the following pages carry graphic references to heroin, beer, peyote, wine, codeine, marijuana, port, LSD, mescaline, vodka and cocaine. But as surely as they confess his addiction to drugs, they attest his addiction to literature. The title 'Things Exactly as They are' comes from Wallace Stevens's long poem 'The Man With the Blue Guitar', itself inspired by Picasso's painting *The Old Guitarist*. 'The Joker' alludes to the supervillain of the Batman comic strip. The words 'Human voices reach us/ and we drown' in 'They Say You are Marching Again' echo the last line of Eliot's 'The Love Song of J. Alfred Prufrock'. 'A Message to Hemingway' incorporates quotations from his short story 'A Clean, Well-Lighted Place' (the first two stanzas) and the novel *A Farewell to Arms* (verses 3-6). 'Once Upon a Time' looks like an extrapolation of the popular anti-war slogan of the Sixties counterculture 'make love not war'. However, the historicity of the title, the opening gambit of many a folk tale, alerts us to a much wider cultural perspective: the body of the poem is a sprightly paraphrase of *Lysistrata*, by the ancient Greek dramatist Aristophanes. 'San Quentin's Stranger' is an Americanization of the second half of Camus's existential masterpiece *L'Etranger*, which is known in the UK as *The Outsider* but as *The Stranger* in the USA. The Korean War incident described in 'I Remember the Time' is given added poignancy by the title's glancing invocation of three favourite anthology pieces: 'Stanzas on Revisiting Shrewsbury' by John Hamilton Reynolds (beginning, 'I remember well the time, the sweet school-boy time'); Winthrop Mackworth Praed's 'I Remember, I Remember'; and Thomas Hood's 'I remember, I remember'. The ironic interplay between poem and title is two-way: for if the slaughter described undercuts these schoolroom classics for sentimentalizing childhood, they in turn reproach a military culture that brutalizes youth. In all these cases, the beauty lies in the fact that the poems still make sense to readers who miss the citations – though, admittedly, not as much sense.

Such ubiquitous use of allusion problematizes the naïve view of Wantling as a verse autobiographer telling it straight. On occasion the citation is so blatant as to resemble Surrealist *objet trouvés* or Marcel Duchamp 'readymades', as with the posthumously published *7 on Style* written as class-aids for his students at Illinois State University. 'Style 1' is quarried from the following paragraph of *The Theatre of the Absurd* by the drama critic Martin Esslin:

> When Beckett is asked about the theme of *Waiting for Godot*, he some-
> times refers to a passage in the writings of St Augustine: 'There is a
> wonderful sentence in Augustine. I wish I could remember the Latin.
> It is even finer in Latin than in English. "Do not despair: one of the
> thieves was saved. Do not presume: one of the thieves was damned."'
> And Beckett sometimes adds, 'I am interested in the shape of ideas even
> if I do not believe in them.... That sentence has a wonderful shape. It
> is the shape that matters.'

A comparison of the two texts confirms that of the poem's 96 words only four were contributed by Wantling; six come from Esslin; while the remaining 68 are quoted from Beckett, 18 being his Englishing of Augustine's Latin. Apart from those four words – Sam, sd, then, he – Wantling's contributions are: some minor omissions and contractions; the capitalizing of the word 'shape' in two of its three usages; and, crucially, the lineating of the original prose. Similarly, 'Style 7' is Wantling's synthesis of the obituaries for the Chilean poet and politician Pablo Neruda, who had just died of cancer having first witnessed the CIA-backed overthrow of the Allende government he served. As T.S. Eliot said: 'immature poets imitate; mature poets steal'.

Wantling's literary kleptomania is also apparent in his use (and abuse) of traditional forms like the sonnet, the sestina, syllabics, the epigram and the haiku. Twenty-two of the latter are included in the present selection, all but one of which adhere to the original Japanese limit of seventeen syllables. Conversely, only 'The Fix' distributes those syllables in the regulation sequence of 5, 7, 5. Indeed, the majority of Wantling's versions employ four, five or six-lines in place of the mandatory triplet. Some obey tradition by keying their content to the changing seasons, beginning 'Spring rains return' or 'secret/ silent/ winter'. Others flout nature to brilliant effect: 'San Quentin 1' and 'San Quentin 2' use the constrictions of the form to embody prison-yard constrictions. Following the entire chain is like listening to John Coltrane's fifty-minute extemporization on Rogers and Hammerstein's song 'My Favorite Things': in both cases, the artist displays his mastery by adopting a restrictive template and then ingeniously and repeatedly escaping it.

These elements of humour, allusion, irony, redaction, collage and ventriloquism (Wantling quoting Esslin quoting Beckett quoting Augustine) frustrate lazy conflations of author and protagonist: Wantling constructs the poems; the poems construct their narrators. 'Pusan Liberty' is one of the finest English language poems to come out of the Korean conflict, comparable to the best First World War poetry in its perception of contending soldiers as alike victims of their respective political and military authorities. The poem offers a clear example of the way Wantling's note of alienated authenticity is artistically constructed rather than being a 'true' account of his personal experience vomited direct upon the page. What convinces us of the poem's veracity is the psychological extremity of the situation, the protagonist buying and shooting up heroin and then selling some on to the Chinese enemy. The poem's acknowledgement, even as it establishes the momentary camaraderie of '3 angry boys lost in the immense/ absurdity of War and State', of the narrator's betrayal of his 'sudden/ friends' by over-charging them for their fix seems like an earnest of psychological candour. Yet that use of the word 'absurdity' when describing the situation the three 'boys' find themselves in, invoking as it does Camus' essay *Le Mythe de Sisyphe* (*The Myth of Sisyphus*), in which the existentialist view of the absurdity of the human condition was given definitive formulation, might be interpreted as a sign, not of the poem's veracity, but of its literariness – or, if you prefer, its fictiveness. It is noticeable that the protagonist is given no name, less a portrait of the artist than a fictional Everyman. Besides, no evidence has come to light that our poet, like his narrator, had a 'girl-wife & child' in Korea; nor that he was already addicted to heroin – that came later, in the USA not Korea, in peacetime not war; nor even that he experienced front line combat. The emotional force of the poem is not the result of Wantling baring his soul but of Wantling baring his technique.

All of this talk of his literary style might seem to contradict 'Poetry', which proposes that poetic effects like 'consonance and assonance and inner/ rhyme' are rendered 'kind of phoney' by the shocking reality of prison life. The piece begins:

> I've got to be honest. I can
> make good word music and rhyme
>
> at the right time and fit words
> together to give people pleasure

and even sometimes take their
breath away...

But then goes on to suggest that this 'word music' is beggared by a murder in the San Quentin exercise-yard, ending with the question:

what could consonance or assonance or
even rhyme do to something like that?

However, the very art and life which the poem seems to separate are bound together in a complex pun: the poet says he can write well enough to take the reader's 'breath away'; the incident which purports to expose such skill as phoney describes Ernie literally taking Turk's 'breath away' by stabbing him fatally in the lung; and the episode is so effectively described that the reader is, indeed, left breathless, aghast at the swiftness and futility of the killing. The second half of the poem is not a negation of the first, but an exemplification of it.

Hence, the terrific spinal column of monosyllabic words ending in 't' that, vertebra by vertebra, provides the poem with its hidden backbone: *got-right-fit-it-won't-fact-that-can't-out-get-cat-what-gut-shirt-caught-bright-just-shit*. Many of these are pure rhymes (*fit-it-shit*) whose density increases rather than diminishing as the poem closes upon the murder scene. Much the same is true of the other poetic effects that are supposedly redundant in the San Quentin exercise-yard: consonance (the use of words with identical consonants but different vowels), far from being dispensed with, is conspicuous in the *got-get-gut* series; and assonance (vowel identity in words whose consonants differ) is equally prominent in the *how-down-now* and *make-tray-laid* sequences. Finally, note how Wantling avoids end-stopping thirty of the thirty-four lines in the poem. Lacking terminal punctuation, the lines end in an unwritten question:

And Turk (*and Turk did what?*)
pulled out his stuff and shanked (*and shanked what?*)

Ernie in the gut only Ernie had a (*had a what?*)
metal tray in his shirt. Turk's (*Turk's what?*)

shank bounced right off him and (*and what?*)
Ernie pulled his stuff out and of (*and of what?*)

course...

The stranglehold of syntax upon lineation is broken, the reader being propelled down the page by the need to conclude each sentence. This breathless series of enjambments structurally enacts the poem's central pun upon the taking away of breath, the reader's precipitous but staccato progress being such as to leave one gasping. And the final sentence offers no closure, the poem ending with a rhetorical question whose implied answer (that consonance, assonance and rhyme can play no part in describing the murder) is, as we have seen, the wrong one! This is poetic mastery, a source of exquisite pleasure.

The fame of many distinguished poets (Robert Herrick, Andrew Marvell, Walter de la Mare) rests on a handful of perfectly achieved poems. However erratic, however self-destructive, Wantling has more than enough masterpieces to mean that his reputation ought to be assured. Yet all his individual collections have long fallen out of print. He is excluded from every one of the standard anthologies of modern American poetry. His place as the pre-eminent American poet of the Korean War has yet to be properly recognized. The greatness of his prison writings (he is the Poet Laureate of San Quentin) and of his drug poems is scanted, presumably because of the opprobrium surrounding these subjects. He is even excluded from the Beat canon where he merits a place of honour. This Tangerine Press edition is therefore a wonderful opportunity to redress the balance. Open the goddamn door and say hello!

JOHN OSBORNE
HULL, ENGLAND

A man's work is nothing but this slow trek to rediscover, through the detours of art, those two or three great and simple images in whose presence his heart first opened.

ALBERT CAMUS

In the Enemy Camp

Selected Poems 1964-74

The Awakening

I found the bee as it fumbled about the ground
Its leg mangled, its wing torn, its sting
   gone
I picked it up, marvelled at its insistence
   to continue on, despite the dumb brute
   thing that had occurred
I considered, remembered the fatal struggle
   the agony on the face of wounded friends
   and the same dumb drive to continue
I became angry at the unfair conflict suffered
   by will and organism
I became just, I became unreasoned, I became
   extravagant
I observed the bee, there, lying in my palm
I looked and I commanded in a harsh and angry shout—
   STOP THAT!
Then it ceased to struggle , and somehow suddenly
   became marvellously whole, and it arose
   and it flew away
I stared, I was appalled, and I was overwhelmed
   with responsibility, and I knew not where to begin.

A Message to Hemingway

You explored the Nada Y
Pues Y Nada Y Pues Y Nada

Y Nada Y Nada & you faced
that down, accepted it &

went on from there & you
found that all the beauti-

ful words in all the beautiful languages were obscene

besides the names of towns
the battles fought, the

number of men killed & you
stood there in the rain

listening, muttering Shit
Shit, fuck the bastards, I'll

get it down, get it down true
& you did that in your *A Farewell*

To Arms & later in your *The
Sun Also Rises* & then you got

a little older & a little
lazier & you forgot to believe

in yourself but now if a million idiot words of comment

are written on your later
failures & your clouded death

we can never yet forget those
first stories nor those 2 novels

nor the way you worked until
sometimes after you put it down

so true you knew it was so true
that your head held a hot true

flame & you ran outside shaking
your head & shouting yes yes yes

my god yes, that's the way it was!

Death is a Dream

Death
is a dream full of
     laughter
where
mad objects called
     life
     intrude.

Without Laying Claim

without laying claim
to an impossible innocence
I must tell you how
in the midst of that crowd
we calmly pulled the pins
from six grenades
mumbling an explanation
even we didn't believe
& released the spoons
a lump in our throats

The Korean

stood stiffly pressed against
    the wall
arms folded
              staring
...flinched
when the bullet sang
                    fell
outward into the cobblestoned
    court
one too many holes in his head
for stealing from Americans

Pusan Liberty

the 6 x 6 bounces me down the
washboard roads, I see the

sun-eaten walls of Korea, my
girl-wife & child in a mud &

straw hut back in Taegu & here
I am meeting the SEAL as he

sits on his roller-skate cart
minus arms & legs but beneath

his ass a million $'s worth
of heroin—I make my buy

walk through the 10,000 cam-
era market-place, jeeps for

sale, people for sale, I'm
even for sale as I find the

porch of Cutie's suckahatchi
house & fix, sitting in the

sun on the adobe veranda, the
2 Chinese agents come around

to make their buy, 2 young
boys, they're hooked bad & I

charge them too much—we sit
there & fix, I fix again, the

so-called Enemy & I, but just
3 angry boys lost in the immense

absurdity of War & State sudden
friends who have decided that

our hatred of Government exceeds
the furthest imaginable limits

of human calculation.

Don't Shoot

'Don't shoot!' she
screamed, & as the dark
shadowed figure clicked
back the pistolhammer
twice I muttered Sheeeit...
I snapped off the set &
Ruthie hollered in from
the kitchen—Whatsamatter
Genius, too deep for you?
& I put Miles'
                    SKETCHES OF
SPAIN on the stereo & we
had popcorn that night, 7-
up, & made love on the
livingroom rug
then when Ruthie was sleep-
ing, I read an old letter
from my first wife, wrote
a poem about her & the years
in L.A. & the narcotics, &
wondered about that old man
whose skull we'd had to
fracture to take his lousy
$83 that one bad sick
time, wondered if he'd
lived, if he'd ever just
loved & lived simply & with
total thanks as I had this
night...

Heroin

what
I remember of the good times...

high, once I ate 3 scoops of ice-cream
high it was the greatest
greater than the Eiffel tower
greater than warm sex, sleepy
early on a morning

and once, high...
so high I never reached that peak
again, happy my wife & I
lie coasting beside a small pond
in an impossibly green park
under a godblue sky
birds swimming V's on the smokey water
the sun weaving patterns through the
leaves, small shadows swimming on
her face & arms
& she says—Baby, I feel so *fine*.

so fine...
that was twice
the rest was nothing, even
less
the pain's still there

Poetry

I've got to be honest. I can
make good word music and rhyme

at the right times and fit words
together to give people pleasure

and even sometimes take their
breath away—but it always

somehow turns out kind of phoney.
Consonance and assonance and inner

rhyme won't make up for the fact
that I can't figure out how to get

down on paper the real or the true
which we call life. Like the other

day. The other day I was walking
on the lower exercise yard here

at San Quentin and this cat called
Turk came up to a friend of mine

and said Ernie, I hear you're
shooting on my kid. And Ernie

told him so what, punk? And Turk
pulled out his stuff and shanked

Ernie in the gut only Ernie had a
metal tray in his shirt. Turk's

shank bounced right off him and
Ernie pulled his stuff out and of

course Turk didn't have a tray and
caught it dead in the chest, a bad

one, and the blood that came to his
lips was a bright pink, lung blood,

and he just laid down in the grass
and said Shit. Fuck it. Sheeit.

Fuck it. And he laughed a long
time, softly, until he died. Now

what could consonance or assonance or
even rhyme do with something like that?

All the Fucking Time

All the fucking time
I was in San Quentin
I kept remembering my
stinking bitch of an
old lady and how I'd
rode the beef for her
and how she'd stopped
writing in 9 months
and served papers and
shacked up with some
Chicano from East L.A.
who was a pimp & on
parole from Q himself
and let me tell you
Jack, it was *good* to
lie there in my top
bunk while my cellie
snored & think of all
the ways I'd *do* them
when I hit the streets
and I tell you Jack IT
GOT SO GOOD TO ME I MORE
THAN ONCE *COME* behind
it—then after 5½ years
I got my date then 2 weeks
later I got the letter
from my Chick's mother
saying You remember
how Shirley & you caught
Hepatitis off that dirty
needle, well she got it
again somewhere and I
don't know quite how to
tell you this but last
Tuesday at 7 pm she died
In L.A. General Hospital
and the Public Assistance

people has placed your
son in a Foster Home and
want you to sign Adoption
papers...
Like I've been on the bricks
almost 6 months now and tried
it with about 10, 12 chicks
and can't cut the mother-
fucking mustard Shit I wonder
what's wrong?

from Sestina To San Quentin

for Ken Whelan

Do you remember now?
How the grey and green walls rose invincible about us?
How we raised our eyes to the sheer heights climbing to
    a final pinnacle perspective
Until high, high off over our heads we saw the
Sun-stricken gun-towers, the archer-turrets of ancient
    castles?
And how, scudding by the turrets, scudding through the
    child-blue sky
Great puffed balls of popcorn clouds went tumbling by, the
Chaste being chased by reflected crimsons from a dying
    sun?

Do you remember how the gulls went wheeling and crying
    their shrill plaintive cries?
How they spun down in tightened spirals to spy upon us
    and climb again?
How their wings pounded the air until, catching a rising
Current of warmth they spread their wings wide and were
    free, free and still, serene, hanging
Poised then swiftly gliding as the chance quick current
Drifted them off over the deep blue waters of the bay?

In the Enemy Camp

It looks as if I'm to
spend my life in enemy
camps. 2 months ago I
finally got free of San
Quentin and the Calif
Dept of Corrections—
after 5½ years. So I
came to Peoria to free-
load and Write. Now for
2 months I haven't heard
Art Pepper or Gerry
Mulligan or Jimmy Giuffre
—not even on the radio
Farmer Bill but no Charlie
Mingus or John Handy. To-
day I got funny looks when
I walked around town in
my go-aheads. The whore-
houses have been closed
since 1953 and when I
offered to eat a girl
up she looked shocked
and asked me if I've
seen a doctor about my
sex problem. The boys
don't play my game
either. I can't find
one lousy joint of weed
and nobody here ever
heard of Peyote. The cops
are polite and the negroes
humble. I'm thinking of
moving on. How far to
the next enemy camp?

It's Cold for August

it's cold for August
& it's been raining now
for 3 days & nights
a vague unease has
settled over many in
this place
         unease
denied in the usual
manner, things going
on as usual

   when I see
the people playing
golf in a Sunday rain
  see them
flocking to a small
sad circus & being
gaily cheated, peeping
small sad peeps of
counterfeit joy, as if
the grand old days had
   never ended
            or I
notice the insects are
gone, the ladybugs
  the lightning bugs
  the grasshoppers &
   the ants
& how few birds
returned this year

I remember the famed
mount of ancient days, how
the volcano came like the
  Voice of God, burying the
town as it went about

its daily tasks
& then remember the
Hiroshima volcano, the
one erupting over
    Nagasaki
& I walk alone through
a deserted park, wishing
I could leave with the
birds, or like the black
dog before me, pissing
on the nearest public
    statue

Two Haiku

We have ever known
it would end...

Yet always before
we are ready?

If only life
would remain thus
the dawn
the cool grass
I inside you

One Short Poem

Sweetest of what I leave behind
is the flesh of a girl, after that
a dawn sky save for the
     Morning Star
but also an icy beer, a midsummer after-
noon, someone to laugh with me

Who's Bitter?

when Judge Lynch
denied probation
& crammed that 1-14
up my ass
for a First Offence
I giggled

when Dr God
stuck 7 shocktreatments
to me
for giving my chick
in Camarillo
2 joints
I laughed aloud

now
when the State of Illness
caught me bending over
2 jugs of Codeine
cough medicine
& charged me w/Possession
& Conspiracy
I shrieked
in idiot joy

a bit worried
they all inquired
—What are you Wantling?
—A goddam Masochist?
I, between hilarious gasps
O howled—No,
—I'm a Poet!
—Fuck me again!

Letter from Kickapoo (pop. 250)

I'm
hiding out
from the heat here

this time
they want me
for Living without Believing
for Working without Slavery
Playing without Patterns
and Loving without Misery

please don't give me away?

it was 5 am

it was 5 am &
the only station coming thru
was this 50,000 watt clear-
channel out of Austin &

this jesus freak got on for
someplace called Ambassador
College &
for over an hour he revealed
how long hair
drugs
youthful disrespect for the
Father, for the old standards
& beliefs
& for authority
was destroying the traditional
family unit   was undermining
Democracy   &
threatening our survival
as a great nation

I lit a joint &
thought how grateful I was
that he was right   &
thought how there was
still hope

Ah, History!

I've fought this thing with silken hate
these drumbeat lines impale our lives
each pitch insisting THIS IS HISTORY!
this whip which keeps us tame
that puts us through our pace
that keeps us trained
and this is all I can tell you
all I can tell you is this:

I was born
I will die
I am not contained

yes, I've argued this
with broken tongue
yet nothing changed

now, upon this awkward ball of Mud
at certain times I see
despite the poison raging through my blood
all
all is ecstasy

Ah, Baby ...

Ah Baby, don't pout. the game
is a good one. because today
there's no one left worth hating
because today you are my Sister
& because today is a day to
love each other. forget that
you always want me to be doing
     what I'm not doing
& not doing what I'm doing
     forget that
it's no way to do a life. I don't
     know where I've been
I don't know where we're going, I
don't even know the name of this
     game
but because the red sun rose
     this morning, because
you laughed & said 'Welcome Home!'
     because
I'm alive now, we're alive now
     right   here
       & now
we've already won

The Joker

on Acid one time
I saw God all in
a pulse of pure light
   another time
I saw a little man
tiny body
enormous misshapen
boil-red head
nose full of pockmarks
mouth twisted into a
contemptuous leer
pointing at me and laughing
was this not God, too?
   Light...
   Leer...
   God...
it all swings, doesn't it?

Her White Body

if you had any sense
she sd
You'd know we're going
to die soon, glaring
as I tied up
Yes, I sd & hit my ante-
cobital, that's why I'm
fixing

and who

and who
but we two
were truly sick
    WITHDRAWAL
the first time
is unbelievable
is panic
is hysteria without
end for one
knows not if
the pain will
end or will not end
        will become
more intense
until...

& *She* says
—Boost some
cameras from where
you work, climb in
the
    window

& I say
—No, think
of fingerprints
  for I am
most cautious
no—I am A
    FRAID
    the first taste
of the true
coward / Ah.

—Fuck you
then punk, she
says, my Wife, 'Punk'

she says, & I take it
because of coward's
guilt

—Fuck you
then, and she slams
              the door
elbowing into the black
raincoat &
              is gone

    10.30
    11.00
    midnight

and with the stroke
of the witching hour, my
beautiful bitch returns
    —kicks the
door twice
              'Bill!'
& I open to
her laugh, her
loving armful of
cameras, cameras
              cameras

—Let's go
score, Baby
    softly spoken
but pain & anticipation
bring us again
              to laughter
& love again

A short treatise on love and perversion with psychoanalytic overtones

my father slept
my mother wept
and I became the horned goat between them

A metaphysical promise from one who is quite angry that all dreams soon become nightmares

i'll kill you, God
first chance i get

We Make a Deal

we make a deal
I don't drink for 24hrs
they'll get me home
Naima gives me her Mescaline
& we smoke our last 2 joints
going over the Golden Gate
bridge, then
standing on the flight deck
Jim & Irv & Naima & young John
chant   OM...
loving me off to Chicago
but
when the seatbelt sign
flashes off
I run to the washroom
bolt the door
puke & shiver
drop my last downer
sink back into my
cabin class seat, &
somewhere over Kansas City
hit a heavy pocket of
flashbacks
step out of myself
stand there
staring down
at the heap
on my seat
the cold sweat on its face
stinking of
weeks-old wine, the
grime, the
greasy tics & tremors
& I say to myself

—Theres yr body
   baby, now
   love it or leave it
   nows yr last chance
& I do not suffer preaching gladly
but
I wish you were here too
standing beside me
miles above the twitching
earth
staring down at Kansas or
China or Chicago as
the sun chases dying shadows
across our poisoned land
& I take yr hand & point down
& preach a bit, say to you
—Theres our body
   baby, now
   love it or leave it
   nows our last chance

Sometimes When I Get Paranoid

sometimes, when I get paranoid
and am certain the Earth is merely
a laboratory where
extra-galactic technicians put us
through our stimulus/response paces
I come out the other side
& excited now, realise
So What?
I mean, you can swing on it anyway
if you don't let it get in the way
but then I think of *the* Swing
I lost it, as they say, on the swing
when I was 7
O I know the Golden Age
is a farce, but at 7 you
accept the improbability of it all
and our knees touched
as we soared
which makes me a Romantic
but at 7 you accept the improbability
you soar, when
your knees touch in the swing

7 to this place is a long time
which is probably why I haven't
written any love poems
in a long time
& why revolution isn't the answer
either

San Quentin's Stranger

In Death Row's dim undersea
light, he watched them
preparing the Pellet, testing
the cables & pulleys, & it
held his terror of the dawn

He read again
her last letter
& knew his last bond
with life
was this memory
of a girl's cool hand

During the next hour
a chaplain came
to offer an empty hope
But he would not allow
that futile prayer, that
wasted hour

In the last half-hour
his despair shifted
& in that slight pivotal
point he embraced
the life which consumed him
found there was no fate
he could not surmount
with scorn

HEROIN HAIKUS

The Fix

Give me the moment
that will join me to myself
in a mad embrace.

Los Angeles—1

Full moon.
I bolt my door—
     as up the ancient stairs
     cocaine shadows glide...

Los Angeles—2

I bring a can of weed.
Grady brings pills and peyote.
Party Time!

The Bust

A knock, the door
   flumps down.
Shotguns, the heat screams—
   Freeze, you dirty dopers!

County Jail—1

Finally, the count is clear.
    The lights dim.
Bugles sound—
    a cockroach charge!

County Jail—2

Sick call.
   O heroin god!
For my withdrawal pains—
   ten aspirin.

County Jail—3

Four months pass...
   At last,
The D.A. asks me to
   plead guilty, save time.

Visiting Day

My wife!
I tell her I got the joint.
She is too loaded
    to answer.

San Quentin—1

First day on the Big
Yard. Two shankings, a
   race riot
        and no letter.

San Quentin—2

Walk slow
drink a lot of water.
      My Dear John is
four years old today.

It was Tuesday Morning

It was Tuesday morning
I was flunking out of school
The February sun was hazy
I went to bed with 2 jugs of white port
to drink myself asleep
but I kept flashing back to the day before
...I kept letting my dog off her chain
& she kept running out in the road to
chase the gasoline tanker
& she kept slipping under the rear wheels
& she kept yelping with surprise as she
sat in the road with her guts hanging out
between her back legs & her eyes
never stopped looking at me with shamed surprise
as if she'd got caught shitting on the rug
& then the sun was bouncing off her eyes
like a handball off a blank concrete wall
flicker / flicker
death
flicker
Then Dan came over with some Mesc & Acid
I dropped 2 caps & a tab & waited but it
started doing some real bad things
So I borrowed a nickel from Dan & jumped
on my bike
It took 2 months to ride the half-mile
to the liquor store & the fifth of 100-proof
vodka kept muttering under its breath
during the 100-mile ride home
things like
—We're going to get you Wantling, your
number is really up this time, Baby...
& to stop its goddam muttering I slammed
its neck against a bus-stop bench & chug-a-lugged
it but it kept muttering, stupidly, instead of
warm there was an icy thing in my belly, muttering...

& the flashbacks were coming on faster now
like some strobe-light gone mad with prophecy
It was *me* in the road with my guts hanging out
& I was hung up on the pain, the shame, the
surprise in my eyes
I couldn't see the road anymore...
Maybe my bike knew the way home by itself
Anyway, I was there, back in the bedroom
but the muttering was louder now
nervous, ugly
& I went for all the old pills I'd stashed
when I wasn't sure what they were
There was half a handful, all colors
& I dropped them & wished the sweat
would stop running down my back legs
& hoped I wouldn't puke till the pills
began to work
But after a while things started coming out
of the corners
muttering
coming straight for me
& I looked down, curious, to see the
dot inside my left wrist
widen into a black rotting ring
& then the artery jumped out
& started gushing blood 2 feet into the air
Then the blood turned to pus
& the muttering steadied into a loud hum now
crackling with shrieks & static
& beneath it somewhere there was a drum
There were 10,000 steel-heeled boots
Stomping out a refrain
—Now now now now it's your turn now...
& I guess some of the shrieks were mine
for 2 days later my wife found me under
the bed curled up in a ball, covered with shit
& vomit
But here I am now fairly calm
full of tranquillisers & group therapy

It evidently wasn't my turn after all
What I wonder is, why all the hassle?
Why all the bullshit?
I never wanted to be a poet anyway
I'd carry a lunchbox like everybody else
If only the muttering would stop

Actually

actually
to sum up 35 years
Billie Holiday
is the onle sane person
I ever met
& shooting heroin
the only sane thing
I ever did

Essay on Being 35

If I could only
remember how to laugh...

I can't even look a young girl
straight in the legs anymore

& mostly I sit down to piss, now

I taught my wife to masturbate
so I could sleep more
or at least lay there
& stare at the wall

She cries while she does it

After 8 days in bed
I developed athlete's foot
I wonder if I have some Jewish blood?

My mother is worried about me
I wish I were still addicted to heroin
things were much simpler, then

If I could snap out of this funk
I'd have enough energy
to kill myself
but if I had the energy
I wouldn't feel like it

Jesus, life is complicated
I wonder if I have some Jewish blood?

What I need is
a good young piece of ass
but what would I do with it?

I'll bet you think this
is one of those *funny* poems
It's funny, alright

Today I forgot how to cry
Every day, in every way
I'm getting flatter & flatter

HELP

Dreams are Cages

Dreams
are cages
within which we
observe the cages
    without

Once Upon a Time

women finally got good
& sick & tired of wars

sons, lovers, fathers
dead, sacrificed to the
Great God Politics

& with singleness of
purpose making all
women as one woman
upon a given signal
they told their lovers
this:

NO MORE COCK FOR YOU
            DADDY
IF YOU GO FOR THE
OKEE DOKE AGAIN

the men, well, they
laughed good-naturedly

after all, women are
women, ha ha, my old
lady won't last one
hot night, ha ha
but 6 months later
scarce indeed was
the laughter

some men brought out
the latent homosexual
in themselves, some
suffered in silence

but the greater part
of mankind became
ever more impatient
& ever more wistful
& one day a meeting
was called which
turned out to be
very short indeed
& that was the day
the wars ended

I Think of Those Once Great

I think of those once great
of those who once loved
of those who now love
of those who didn't count
I think of the cowards
   the thieves
    the pimps of culture
    the whores of art
the killers & their victims
& those now brave & great
  (history has no tears)
& I can find no fault

Everyone
   always
      does their best
the only rule is
     don't put anyone down
we all
  always
    do the best we can
  (who does not fear themselves?)

& I have a friend
     keeps
a Thompson in his closet
me, I love knives
     knives
& grenades
  (O.K., history has no tears)
Love
  but carry a club

Sure

sure
I'd like to love
altogether & believe
absolutely in non-
violence & make
this a world
where children
no longer suffer
& die
where deer
can graze in our
backyards &
'passport' is a
forgotten anachronism
where everyone
understands Camus
& Schweitzer...

but
can you be a
pacifist
after you've killed
too many
& if one is too many
where do I stand
with *my* score?

what I wouldn't
give to go back, to
start all over

and you?

I Remember the Time

I remember the time
Black got it
incoming knocked him back
into a snowbank
buried him
he was Missing-in-Action
    all winter

spring thaw & we were
back on the same hill &
the Lt. stumbled on him
cracked his shin-bone on
Black's helmet & looked

down at Black, preserved like
a fresh side of beef
    all winter

'You Sonofabitch' he said
to Black's stiff corpse

'You Sonofabitch, if you'd
been more careful I
wouldn't hafta write
all those Goddam letters'
'You Sonofabitch' & he spit

but I'd seen his eyes
watering before he looked
straight up into the sun.

Korea 1953

Endless weeks of zero
A lurking bunker on a barren
    hill
Waiting to receive our orders
    Probe, Capture, Kill
As if one must recompense in
      limbo
For each probe which lacked
         all sense

In that strange war that was not
a war, that came to us too late
When we enjoyed sanctioned
     Murder
And sought the purge of murderous
           hate
We found a certain inner logic to
        our violence
A game in which each player and
    his mate
        understood all rules
(each sensing his brother's center)
And at the expense of this—genius of
          fools

One might purge oneself
    so clean
That love would come to our dead
    winter
        for one cannot hold
          an inner void
And if one's hate is utterly
           purged
One's intuition told
    that love could enter
And we, bold, would become merged
    with our idiot other selves
And returned to time of childhood
          Grace
Yet we became
as a pack of maddened dogs that race
    caged, snarling, for the hand
      which flings
The one small piece of rancid meat
in the center of our corrupted sand
...And the single victor cannot eat
The prize before dying in his blood's
    slow-cooling heat

Harlan's Back From Nam

told me how these new young
lieutenants are real
degenerates
told how he came back from
patrol with a necklace of
left ears & said
—Look lieut, heres
6 more gooks wont bother us
no more
& how the lieut just stared
mumbled—Wow. Great. The
Corps really made a
Man outa you. Yeah
Harlan said if he hadna been
a lieutenant he'd a punched
him out
said
he requested a transfer
to another outfit, said
they sent him home instead
Listen! Godamnit
all those *words* you just read
is pure bullshit, Baby
you weren't there & besides you're
some kinda degenerate yourself
& that little draft-dodgin'
commie punk some big brother
You see what I mean about Harlan?
I guess I'll stay in college
Psych major
go on to grad school
move away from this town
before Harlan gets in trouble
gives us all a bad name

The Day War was Declared

Well, it somehow seems
sort of funny, now, if

it was tragic to begin
with it's grown funny

with time, like a dead
old man's red underwear

like the way Red China
finally got into the U.N.

...most of us past 40
remember the vicious

irony of the day They
struck, Dec. 7 again

just like back in '41
and the humor of the

whole mess struck later
years later, for the 10

or 20 of us that were
left to begin civili-

zation all over again
I mean, it was all over

dead, quiet, and over
before War was declared

Politics

last night we were all
toking up down at the

YMCA when this Wolf ran
in, began slashing at

Jack's calves & ankles
got him hamstrung, and

was dragging him out the
door when I stopped it

with a good left hook to
the snot-locker. Well,

I phoned a doctor from
the hall then went back

in to finish my joint
but Carlos and a few

others had grabbed up
rifles and a case of

molotov cocktails and
set off to Missionary

the Wolves. I wouldn't
go & they spit on me as

they filed out the door
Well, shit, where's my

Thompson? A man alone
just ain't got a chance...

Dialogue

Men whose names are great
I must explain
Like you I am human
Being human, I am often weak
Although weak, I more often hate

Like you I am quite vain
Kind only when frightened
Thoughtful only when necessary
Humble only in pain

Men whose names are great
I am so much everything
you detest within yourselves
I offer myself as a bad example
for edification of your masses
for crucifixion on your cross of State

Can you do other than accept?

They Say You are Marching Again

In the clinging jungle heat
even a bullet burns

a stinging screws into my gut
wetly it spreads, turns
with dull beat
sweats blood down my belly
and the corpsman pretends
—You're OK, be brave!

Water—I must have water!
they give me morphine instead
I vomit, the darkness descends
A jungle my grave?

...wet earth unfolds the dead

They say you are marching again
marching for Peace, against what is wrong
but dollars drown the cries
of women, children, charred alive
Why did you wait so long?

Human voices reach us
and we drown
brother turns on brother
Vietnamese on Viet Cong
while over it all, the
roar of American dollars

Why did you wait so long?

Once There were Children

I hate you, she
said. And, as if

she really were
going to absolve

us both from ever
loving again she

threw her rings
her wedding ring

her ear-rings, her
nose ring and her

ankle-chain at my
long-suffering head

and burst into tears
as if her heart were

being crushed in a
vice. I had seen

this kind of shitty
act before, however

so I turned up the TV
full blast and lit up

my foulest cigar
knocking the ashes

on the rug and allow-
ing my immense erection

to show. It was almost
an hour before she begged

me to come to bed. I
ignored her, for though

she begged me prettily
though she pleaded, she

had waited long and hadn't
sunk to her knees before me.

Therapy

I wanted to destroy this
entire contemporary mess
I'm caught in, the social
lies, the motherfucking
so-called civilization
which seems to lack the
freedom we all crow about
so goddam much, the idiot
middle-class I'm trapped
in by the fact that my
art is ignored, as all
contemporary art is ig-
nored until it is no longer
contemporary, until it is
old and respectable and
safe. Yeah, I wanted to
blow up the world with-
out hurting the people in
it... what a fignewton that
one was. So instead I be-
came a heroin addict, in
the words of the fools and
friends who tried to help
I *internalized* my hatred.
So they got their way, by
god, the long dead years
in prison and the promise
of more to come, the years
spent in psychotherapy and
group therapy all had the
desired effect... I am no
longer a heroin addict and
am no longer in danger of
ever becoming one again
but something dead happened
in these long dead years
something unlocked for in

all the happy bullshit called
'therapy' ...I ceased to
care, I ceased to care about
anything much at all. Now I've got a surplus 20mm.
machine gun and a crate of anti-
personnel grenades hidden in
my closet. I'm just waiting
for the first bad day when
I'll decide to begin...

Things Exactly as They are

Things exactly as they are
Are Paradise
But it's always so quiet
When the crickets die

Two Haiku

Spring rains return.
Disgusted, my pregnant cat
Stalks a frozen sparrow.

Loving, hating one another
I and the world
whirl, share illusions

Dirge in Spring

There
high on a hill
a man plows his field.
The sun warm, the day still
and the air
still also, a shield
for the earth.
                 And below
blind from new birth
hide the young of a hare.
Crouched in the lair
soft, without will
they dream. The doe runs
fast over field, turns
before the plow, urging
the man to take up her dare.
He is blind to her. Without concern
or rancor, he rips the soft dream.
His plow a high scream
in her ear, the doe runs on.
It is not rare
for such to be ripped
from the lair of life.
And the man?

Lemonade 2c

Kathy was my
first customer
naturally, I
turned her on
free
she put her
cool hand in
mine
led me to her
dark & sweaty
cellar
kissed me
Lord, how our
lips trembled
how bitter-sweet
& cool
that lemonade

Haiku

secret
silent
winter

the sound of
snowflakes sifting
down together

2-Man Cell

I sat there on my bunk
& I ask him maybe 8, 10 times
& every time I'd ask him I
had to ask him again
cause I just couldn't believe
his answer
& every time I asked him:
      —Why, Bud?
      —Why
He'd say
      —I just didn't want to
hassle anymore, did you ever
feel like that?
& I wouldn't accept that, I'd
frown like a fool & I'd say
      —Why, Bud?
      —But why, Man? Why?
& he'd just stare at me
through his cigarette
but once he got tired, I guess
of all those questions
& he said
      —Did you ever see so many
cops, Man, for so long a time?
      —That all at once, like, you
just didn't want to hassle? Anymore?
      —You just got tired, allofasudden
& just didn't want to hassle anymore? *You
just didn't feel like hassling anymore?*

That was 7 years ago
I understand now, what he meant. Now

For Ernie Marshall
if He's Still Around

on the streets he'd lived
the baddest western ever made
armed robbery every night
so often that nobody'd ever
heard of him, tho he made
Ring twice, the record book

Ernie, jealous of Oedipus
had three tragic flaws:
he was black
he was intelligent
he really loved to come

I knew him in San Quentin
every morning like prayer
shadowboxing in the Lower Yard
& he had this white kid who
hustled for them
O for a while it was ice-cream
it was starched dungarees every
day, their jacket collars rolled
it was Paranoid Corner, sitting
in the Sun
also there was Bob, a crewcut
guard from Harlan County
used to dogeye Ernie every day
didn't like to see him handle
that kid
—Whats a nigger doing with
sumthin like that anyhow

every morning like prayer
Rage & Color don't mix

The Question Is

—You Pig-Rat, the
Warden sd
—You think yr slick, but
there's another 5 thousand
just like you
out on the Big Yard
We'll get you, we
get 'em all, sooner
or later
What makes you think
yr special? What makes
you think we won't get
you? heh heh
Snuffle heh umm...

—You won't get me, Warden
cause I'm *not* like those
others on the Big Yard
I pity you, you poor squirming
bundle of nerves, I pity
you—*but they hate you*
& pity isn't careless
Hate is

It was worth 10 days
in The Hole to see
his face whiten, his
lips tighten & tremble
More than worth it
The question is, did
they get me?

The Death of Caryl Chessman

Little did i know, then
The price of my revenge
If someone had foretold
Those long years of quiet
        terror and grey steel
I would have shrugged and
        laughed, saying
'A hard price for having my
        way with a virgin.'
Then the long years began
And setting aside my hot
        dreams of glory
I came to understand...

So they bathed my body with
        gas

Time and the City:
Some Seventeen Syllable Comments

1
On the freeway
I follow redglow taillights
To my city of glass

2
I was not here yesterday
also
I will not be here tomorrow

3
Will you please explain this
I hate you
I fear you
I return always

4
The pain of your people
tears my flesh
Still...
There is the hour before dawn

5
I will not be here yesterday
also
I was not here tomorrow

There are a Few Things to Note

there are a few things to note
before I leave
but not many
I haven't learned much in 37 years

1. all governments are eventually appalling
2. pain hurts
3. to eat meat is murder
4. to be without love is inexcusable
5. to love is the most difficult of all

Style 1

Sam Beckett
when asked abt *Godot*
sd
    theres a wonderful
    sentence in Augustine
    I wish I cld remember
    the Latin
    it is even finer in Latin
    than in English:
      "Do not despair;
        one of the thieves was saved
        Do not presume:
        one of the thieves was damned."
& then he sometimes adds:
    I'm interested in the shape
    of ideas
    even if I do not believe in
    them...   That sentence has
a wonderful
            SHAPE   It is
the   SHAPE
           that matters

Style 7

ALIVE, ALIVE

Ah, Pablo. Your name so common, as
your love. Common. Complete. All-
encompassing. Everything delighted
you: a rock. a tree. a bird. a
brown & freckled face. a pear. a
plum. a belt-buckle. Sea-foam on
your tongue. Your woman's smile...

Oh it was acid & swordblade, dew on
a blossom a spiral nebula the hollow
of a tree a leaping fish on fire, a
god of stone the State. There was
hate, there was love & blood but
never an abstraction—everything was
concrete, quivering in duplicity, in
its tender pride & shame. Even the
agony delighted you. It was all
shining all beautiful...

Even the cunning crab of cancer (or
was it junta bullet?) in your brain

Haiku

Nothing
is a gaudy dream
enticing us to
annihilation

Haiku

I don't want to say goodbye
but I think it is being said
for me

Illinois born **WILLIAM WANTLING** joined the US Marines at seventeen years of age and served in the Korea War during 1953. He claimed to have been injured after the jeep he was being transported in ran over a landmine. He received severe burns and was treated with morphine. He was honourably discharged in 1955, having attained the rank of sergeant (aged 20 years). The years immediately following his time in the Marines were spent in California, where he met the woman who would become his first wife, Luana. They soon became addicted to heroin and, to support their growing habit, resorted to petty crime, assaults and robbery. By 1958, Wantling was found guilty of forgery and possession of narcotics and incarcerated at San Quentin Prison for 5½ years. Whilst there, his wife (with their son in tow) divorced him. It was in prison that he first taught himself to write. Following his release in 1963, Wantling returned to Illinois, remarried and, under the G.I. Bill, enrolled at Illinois State University, where he went on to obtain a B.A. and an M.A. in English. As well as publishing a number of collections, Wantling was a regular contributor to literary magazines and anthologies, including an appearance in the twelfth edition of the prestigious *Penguin Modern Poets* series. On completing his studies, the faculty asked him to stay on as a lecturer. Wantling died of heart failure on May 2nd 1974, aged 40 years.

JOHN OSBORNE recently resigned as Director of American Studies at the University of Hull in order to become a full-time writer and artist. His latest book is *Radical Larkin, Seven Types of Technical Mastery* (2014).

THURSTON MOORE is an American musician, writer and publisher best known as singer, songwriter and guitarist of rock band Sonic Youth.

may 2015

This first edition is published as a
trade paperback; there are 126 numbered
and lettered copies, handbound in boards
by Tangerine Press, Tooting, London;
copies with the letters of the author's
surname are additionally housed
in a custom slipcase.